X107770921

EXPLORING COUNTRIES

The Dominican Republic

by Walter Simmons

BELLWETHER MEDIA · MINNEAPOLIS, MN

Note to Librarians, Teachers, and Parents:

Blastoff! Readers are carefully developed by literacy experts and combine standards-based content with developmentally appropriate text.

Level 1 provides the most support through repetition of high-frequency words, light text, predictable sentence patterns, and strong visual support.

Level 2 offers early readers a bit more challenge through varied simple sentences, increased text load, and less repetition of high-frequency words.

Level 3 advances early-fluent readers toward fluency through increased text and concept load, less reliance on visuals, longer sentences, and more literary language.

Level 4 builds reading stamina by providing more text per page, increased use of punctuation, greater variation in sentence patterns, and increasingly challenging vocabulary.

Level 5 encourages children to move from "learning to read" to "reading to learn" by providing even more text, varied writing styles, and less familiar topics.

Whichever book is right for your reader, Blastoff! Readers are the perfect books to build confidence and encourage a love of reading that will last a lifetime!

This edition first published in 2012 by Bellwether Media, Inc.

No part of this publication may be reproduced in whole or in part without written permission of the publisher. For information regarding permission, write to Bellwether Media, Inc., Attention: Permissions Department, 5357 Penn Avenue South, Minneapolis, MN 55419.

Library of Congress Cataloging-in-Publication Data

Simmons, Walter (Walter G.)
 The Dominican Republic / by Walter Simmons.
   p. cm. – (Blastoff! readers: exploring countries)
Includes bibliographical references and index.
 Summary: "Developed by literacy experts for students in grades three through seven, this book introduces young readers to the geography and culture of the Dominican Republic"–Provided by publisher.
 ISBN 978-1-60014-729-6 (hardcover : alk. paper)
 1. Dominican Republic–Juvenile literature. I. Title.
F1934.2.S56 2012
972.93–dc23   2011031193

Printed in the United States of America, North Mankato, MN.

010112   1203

Contents

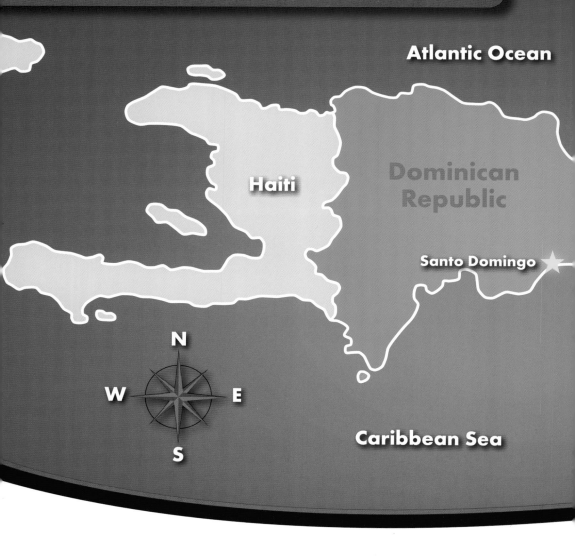

Atlantic Ocean

Haiti

Dominican
Republic

Santo Domingo

N

W   E

S

Caribbean Sea

The Dominican Republic is a small country
between the Atlantic Ocean and the Caribbean
Sea. It covers 18,792 square miles (48,670
square kilometers) and shares a border with Haiti.
Together, the two countries cover the island of
Hispaniola. Puerto Rico, another Caribbean island,
lies to the east of the Dominican Republic.

Puerto Rico

Did you know?

Over 500 years ago, Christopher Columbus was the first European explorer to land on Hispaniola. He thought he had landed in Asia.

Santo Domingo, the capital of the Dominican Republic, faces the Caribbean Sea on the southern coast. Bartholomew Columbus, the brother of Christopher Columbus, helped build this city. It is home to the first hospital ever built in the Americas.

fun fact

The Pomier Caves hold around 6,000 paintings of humans and animals. The Taíno people created these cave drawings that are now up to 2,000 years old.

The Dominican Republic has steep, forested mountains and **fertile** valleys. Four main mountain ranges rise throughout the country. At 10,417 feet (3,175 meters), Duarte Peak in the Cordillera Central is the highest point in the Dominican Republic.

The rivers of the Dominican Republic flow through plains and mountain valleys. Several **tributaries** in the Cibao Valley meet the Yaque del Norte River. This river reaches the sea at Manzanillo Bay. In the southwest, small rivers feed salty Lake Enriquillo. The surface of the lake is 144 feet (44 meters) below **sea level**.

The Cibao Valley runs between the Cordillera Central and the Cordillera Septentrional. It reaches from Manzanillo Bay in the west to Samaná Bay in the east. The valley has a long growing season and is the most fertile area in the Dominican Republic. The weather is dry in the west and humid in the east. The Yaque del Norte and Yuna rivers feed **irrigation canals** that bring water to the fields. The rivers have cut deep banks into the land, where scientists have found **fossils** of many ancient sea creatures.

fun fact

In search of gold and new land, Christopher Columbus sailed to the eastern edge of the Cibao Valley in 1494.

humpback whales

Several rare animal **species** inhabit the Dominican Republic. Rhinoceros iguanas enjoy sunning themselves on rocks and **cacti**. Hutias and solenodons, two mammals **native** to Hispaniola, scurry around in search of food. Crocodiles share the salty waters of Lake Enriquillo with flamingoes and pelicans.

rhinoceros iguana

hutia

flamingo

Off the coasts, **coral reefs** shelter sponges, eels, and many kinds of tropical fish. Crabs, lobsters, shrimp, and barracuda inhabit the warm coastal waters. Whale sharks and dolphins swim in the waters of the Caribbean Sea. Manatees prefer the calm water found around **mangroves**. In early spring, schools of humpback whales can be seen in Samaná Bay.

About ten million people live in the Dominican Republic. This small island country is very crowded. The **ancestors** of most Dominicans came from Europe and Africa. A few Dominicans are related to the Taíno. These **Amerindians** lived on Hispaniola before Europeans arrived.

Spanish is the official language of the Dominican Republic. Many areas of the country speak local **dialects** of Spanish. The people of the Cibao Valley, for example, speak a language that can be difficult for other Dominicans to understand.

Speak Spanish!

English	Spanish	How to say it
hello	hola	OH-lah
good-bye	adios	ah-dee-OHS
yes	sí	SEE
no	no	NOH
please	por favor	POHR fah-VOR
thank you	gracias	GRAH-see-uhs
friend (male)	amigo	ah-MEE-goh
friend (female)	amiga	ah-MEE-gah

Family is very important to Dominicans. Many households include aunts, uncles, cousins, and grandparents. When they become adults, Dominicans often try to live close to their relatives.

Most families in cities live in small houses made of wood or concrete blocks. People get around in taxis, buses, or vans. In the countryside, many people live in homes made of wood and sheet metal. They may lack electricity or running water. Many Dominicans have moved from farms to the city to look for work and to live with other family members.

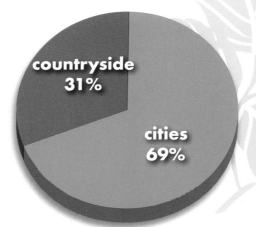

Where People Live in the Dominican Republic

countryside 31%

cities 69%

In the Dominican Republic, children begin their education with one year of preschool. Four primary grades follow. Middle school lasts four years and high school lasts another four. After finishing, students earn a *bachillerato* degree. They may then go to **vocational schools** or universities.

Did you know?

The Dominican Republic has one public university, the University of Santo Domingo. This school opened its doors in 1538. It is the oldest university in the Americas.

In rural areas, going to school can be difficult. Classrooms often lack books, desks, or blackboards. Many students stop after finishing primary school. They cannot afford the costs or have to start working to support their families.

Where People Work in the Dominican Republic

manufacturing 22%

farming 15%

services 63%

Many Dominicans work the land to earn a living. Mines provide gold, silver, and other **minerals**. Los Cacaos, which lies in the south, is one of the world's biggest gold mines. Dominican farmers grow rice, sugarcane, and coffee beans. Some raise cattle, pigs, and chickens.

In the cities, most workers hold **service jobs**. They work in banks, restaurants, and other businesses. Along the coast, many people serve **tourists** in hotels and restaurants. Dominican factory workers use raw materials to make clothing, shoes, and cement. They also produce **refined** sugar and packaged food and drinks.

19

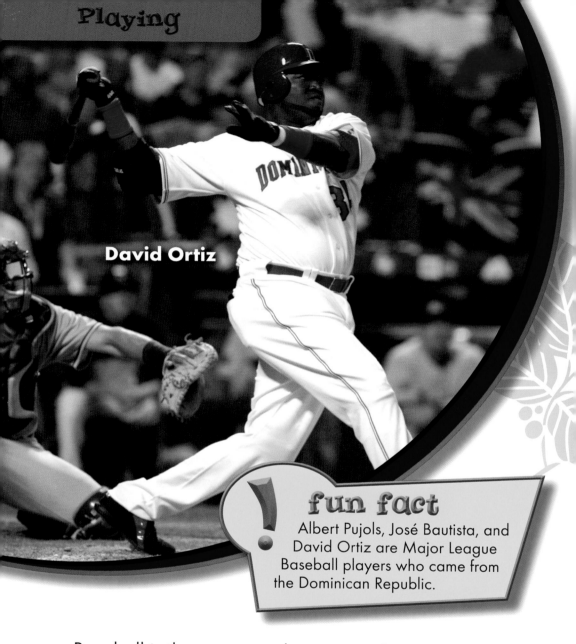

David Ortiz

fun fact

Albert Pujols, José Bautista, and David Ortiz are Major League Baseball players who came from the Dominican Republic.

Baseball is the most popular sport in the Dominican Republic. It arrived from Cuba over 100 years ago. Many Dominican players have made it to Major League Baseball in the United States. The Dominican Republic also has professional basketball and soccer leagues.

Children play tag, jump rope, or kick soccer balls around city streets. Adults enjoy playing checkers and dominoes outside their homes or at neighborhood cafés. In the evening, many people go out to join friends for lively dancing.

Did you know?
Just north of the Cibao Valley is the seaside town of Cabarete. This town has one of the most popular surfing beaches in the Caribbean.

sancocho

! **fun fact**
Dominicans say "*buen provecho*"
before a meal. It means "eat well!"

Dominicans love hot and spicy food. *Sofrito* flavors
many dishes. It is a mixture of oregano, onions, and
chili peppers. Cooks add it to *sancocho*, a stew of
meat or shrimp with vegetables. *Bandera*, which
means "flag," is a dish of white rice, red beans, meat,
and green **plantains**. The colors in this dish remind
Dominicans of their country's flag.

Dominicans enjoy dishes with chicken, pork, or fish. They are often served with onions, corn, beans, or plantains. Mashed plantains make a side dish called *mangú*, which is a favorite any time of day. *Habichuelas con dulce* is a blend of red beans, spices, sugar, and coconut milk. It is a tasty treat after any meal!

mangú

habichuelas con dulce

In the Dominican Republic, each town has a **patron saint**. Saints' days are celebrated with parades, music, and festivals. The Dominican festival of *Carnival* brings people out for a big street party. Throughout February, people wear masks and dance to loud music in parades.

Many holidays in the Dominican Republic celebrate its history. Independence Day takes place on February 27. On this day in 1844, the Dominican Republic freed itself from Haitian rule. **Constitution** Day occurs on November 6. This was the day in 1844 when the country passed its first constitution. Restoration Day on August 16 celebrates freedom from Spanish control in 1865.

fun fact

Three Kings Day falls on January 6 in the Dominican Republic. Kids leave offerings for the three wise men who visited baby Jesus. In the morning, they find gifts in return!

Carnival

Dominicans enjoy many different styles of music. Most styles have a particular dance that goes with them. In many homes, *merengue* plays from the radio. This lively music combines Spanish and African sounds. *Merengue* bands use accordians, pianos, trumpets, and saxophones. A percussion section with maracas and drums gives the music a catchy beat.

Bachata music features guitars and small drums. *Salve* and *palo* songs are played at religious ceremonies. They are characterized by percussion instruments and call-and-response singing. *Reggaeton* has a heavy beat played on a snare drum. The singer delivers fast-spoken lyrics in the style of rap or hip-hop. Dominicans are, like their music, full of energy, rhythm, and fun.

Fast Facts About the Dominican Republic

The Dominican Republic's Flag

The flag of the Dominican Republic features a white cross, two red boxes, and two blue boxes. A crest lies in the center of the flag. The red and blue are colors of Haiti, which once controlled the country. The coat of arms features the motto *Dios, Patria, Libertad,* which means, "God, Country, Freedom."

Official Name: Dominican Republic

Area: 18,792 square miles
(48,670 square kilometers);
the Dominican Republic is the 132nd
largest country in the world.

Capital City:	Santo Domingo
Important Cities:	Santiago, Puerto Plata, La Romana, San Pedro de Macorís, Higüey
Population:	9,956,648 (July 2011)
Official Language:	Spanish
National Holiday:	Independence Day (February 27)
Religions:	Christian (95%), Other (5%)
Major Industries:	farming, manufacturing, mining, services, tourism
Natural Resources:	amber, gold, silver, nickel, mercury, bauxite, iron ore
Manufactured Products:	food products, cars, clothing, chemicals, metals
Farm Products:	corn, sugarcane, cocoa beans, tobacco, rice, beans, plantains, bananas, cattle, chickens, pigs
Unit of Money:	Dominican peso; the peso is divided into 100 centavos.

Glossary

Amerindians—peoples originally from North, South, or Central America

ancestors—relatives who lived long ago

cacti—spiny plants that grow in dry climates

constitution—the basic principles and laws of a nation

coral reefs—structures in coastal waters made up of the bodies of dead corals

dialects—unique ways of speaking a language; dialects are often specific to regions of a country.

fertile—supports growth

fossils—the remains of plants or animals from millions of years ago; fossils are made up of minerals.

irrigation canals—small waterways that bring fresh water to farmland

mangroves—plants that thrive along the shore of a river or the sea

minerals—elements found in nature; gold, silver, and iron ore are examples of minerals.

native—originally from a specific place

patron saint—a saint who is believed to look after a country or group of people

plantains—tropical fruits that look like bananas; plantains are often mashed in the Dominican Republic.

refined—stripped of unwanted parts; Dominican factory workers refine sugarcane into sugar.

sea level—the average level of the surface of the ocean

service jobs—jobs that perform tasks for people or businesses

species—specific kinds of living things; members of a species share the same characteristics.

tourists—people who are visiting a country

tributaries—streams or rivers that flow into larger streams or rivers

vocational schools—schools that train students to do specific jobs

To Learn More

AT THE LIBRARY

Alvarez, Julia. *The Secret Footprints*. New York, N.Y.: Knopf: Distributed by Random House, 2000.

Augustin, Byron. *The Dominican Republic*. New York, N.Y.: Children's Press, 2005.

Temple, Bob. *Dominican Republic*. Broomall, Pa.: Mason Crest Publishers, 2009.

ON THE WEB

Learning more about the Dominican Republic is as easy as 1, 2, 3.

1. Go to www.factsurfer.com.

2. Enter "The Dominican Republic" into the search box.

3. Click the "Surf" button and you will see a list of related Web sites.

With factsurfer.com, finding more information is just a click away.

Index